Step-by-Step
Clay Modelling

Greta Speechley

Heinemann
LIBRARY

www.heinemann.co.uk
Visit our website to find out more information about
Heinemann Library books

To order:

 Phone 44 (0) 1865 888066

 Send a fax to 44 (0) 1865 314091

 Visit the Heinemann Bookshop at www.heinemann.co.uk to
browse our catalogue and order online

Produced by Search Press Limited in Great Britain 2000.
First published by Heinemann Library, Halley Court, Jordan Hill, Oxford
OX2 8EJ, a division of Reed Educational and Professional Publishing Ltd.
Heinemann is a registered trademark of Reed Educational & Professional
Publishing Limited.

OXFORD   MELBOURNE   AUCKLAND   JOHANNESBURG   BLANTYRE
GABORONE   IBADAN   PORTSMOUTH NH (USA)   CHICAGO

Text copyright © Greta Speechley 2000
Photographs by Search Press Studios
Photographs and design copyright © Search Press Limited 2000

The moral right of the proprietor has been asserted.

Originated by Graphics '91 Pte Ltd., Singapore
Printed in Italy by L.E.G.O.

ISBN 0 43111 162 6
04 03 02 01 00
10 9 8 7 6 5 4 3 2 1

British Library Cataloguing in Publication Data

Speechley, Greta
Clay Modelling. – (Step-by-Step)
1.Modeling – Juvenile literature
I.Title
731.4'2

Acknowledgements
The Publishers would like to thank Christie's Images Ltd for permission to
reproduce the photograph on page 5.

Every effort has been made to contact copyright holders of any material
reproduced in this book. Any omissions will be rectified in subsequent
printings if notice is given to the Publisher.

**For my family: my daughter Thea,
who has brilliant ideas; my son Jess,
who has no idea; and my husband
David, who is my 'big' idea!**

*I would like to thank the team at Search
Press, for their help and encouragement in
the making of this book – in particular,
Editorial Director Roz Dace, Editor John
Dalton, Designer Tamsin Hayes and
Photographer Lotti de la Bédoyère.*

. . . .

*The Publishers would like to say a huge
thank you to Jeremy Thornby, Helena
Parkes, Daisy Taylor, Jessika Kwan, Martin
Baker, Emma Tapp, Isobel Hallett and
Amanda Philip.*

*Special thanks are also due to Southborough
Primary School, Tunbridge Wells.*

When this sign is used in the
book, it means that adult
supervision is needed.

REMEMBER!
Ask an adult to help you
when you see this sign.

Contents

Introduction

People have been modelling clay for thousands of years, and pottery fragments have been found that date back as far as 1200 BC. These early pots were baked in bonfires and, because the heat was not very intense, they were very fragile. As a result, only broken pieces of some of the vessels have survived to the present day. Some pots and models have been discovered in tombs and burial places, and you can see wonderful collections of these in many museums. Lots of these ancient vessels were highly decorated with painted figures and animals, which tell wonderful stories of how life used to be. The methods used by craftspeople in those far-off days were simple. Items were hand-modelled and moulded into useful and decorative shapes, just like they are today.

I have taken my inspiration from nature, the world around us, and the simple techniques used by our ancestors to show how easy it is to create colourful and fun models, zany pots, crazy containers and painted tiles. Each project shows a different way of using clay and suggests how you can paint your finished pieces with poster or acrylic paints. You might want to copy each one exactly to start off with, but I am sure that once you have done this, you will want to create your own unique pot or model.

It is a good idea to start using a sketch book or to keep a scrap book so that you can keep a note of the colours you like and use them on your models. Cut out bits of fabric, or snippets from magazines. Think about texture – do you want a smooth finish, or would you prefer a rough surface? Look at pottery and sculpture from different countries and decide which you prefer. My favourite pieces come from Mexico and South America. I love the little figures and curious animals that cover these pots, and they are always painted in such lovely vibrant colours.

I have used air-drying clay for all the projects in this book. It is easy to use and is available from most craft shops. There are quite a few different types. Try to find one that is squidgy when you poke it, rather than being hard. Clay is wonderful to work with – if it does not look quite right, you can just squash it up and start all over again, and it can be used to make almost anything. I am sure you will come up with lots of ideas of your own and have great fun clay modelling. The only limit is your imagination. Have fun!

Note If you have access to a kiln, you can use real clay for all the projects except the solid swinging tiger on pages 16–17. You must ask an adult to use the kiln for you.

Christie's Images Ltd.

No-one knows who made this pottery mythical beast, but they were very skilful because they succeeded in making a simple model look almost life-like. The model, which is about 30cm (11¾in) long, was made in China over 1,500 years ago, when the country was ruled by the emperors of the Han dynasty.

Materials

Apart from clay itself, many of the things you need to get started on clay modelling can be found in your own home. Clay can be messy so it is a good idea to work on a wooden surface or cover your work space with an oilskin cloth.

Air-drying clay is used in this book and you can buy it in packs at craft shops. If it starts to crack and crumble when you are modelling with it, wrap it in clingfilm with a few drops of water and it will soften up. The manufacturer's instructions will tell you how to dry and harden it.

Buy a pack of **plastic modelling tools** from your local art shop. They are cheap and include a variety of shapes for modelling and texturing.

Sponges are used to smooth and finish a clay surface, and to paint finished models.

A **wooden rolling pin** is best for rolling out slabs of clay – clay tends to stick to glass and marble ones. Two **lengths of wood** 0.8cm (5/16in) thick will help you roll out even slabs of clay. Roll the clay out on a piece of **cotton cloth** or an old shirt to create a smooth surface. Use heavily-textured fabric or a piece of hessian if you want to create interesting patterns or textures in the clay.

Clay squeezed though a **garlic press** or sieve makes lovely 'hair' for your models.

Pastry cutters can be used to cut out whole shapes or to create surface patterns on clay.

A small **kitchen knife** is used to cut out clay shapes. Ask an adult to help you do this.

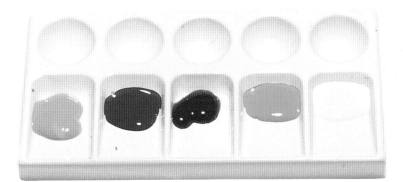

A **palette** is useful for paints, but an old china plate will do just as well. **Acrylic paints** are ideal for painting your models and they come in a huge range of colours. Acrylic paint is tough, it dries to an attractive sheen and it does not need to be varnished. If you decide to use **poster paints** instead, you will need to seal the clay surface with an **acrylic varnish**. Some clays come with recommendations about what paints and varnishes to use, so check the instructions carefully.

Paint can be applied with a **paintbrush** or a sponge. A stiff paintbrush o. old toothbrush can be used to create a random spattered effect.

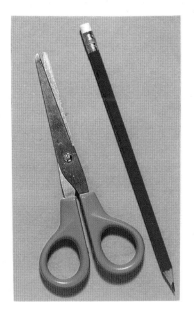

Patterns at the back of the book can be photocopied on to **paper**. Use **scissors** to cut them out. A **ruler** and **pencil** are useful for measuring and drawing straight lines. A pencil can also be used to create lines and texture in the clay.

Clingfilm is used to line moulds to stop the clay from sticking to them.

Techniques

Clay is really easy to work with. You can model straight from a ball of clay, you can coil up long thin sausages, or you can make flat slabs which can be used to build boxes and containers. Practise these techniques before you start the projects.

Pinching out shapes

Note Before you start working on a project, always soften the clay by kneading it in your hands.

This very simple modelling technique is great for making small pots and bowls, and for modelling animals.

Hold a small ball of clay in one hand and press your thumb into the clay to make a hole.

Gently squeeze the clay between your thumb and fingers and work evenly round the ball of clay to open up the shape. Stop from time to time to see how your shape is progressing.

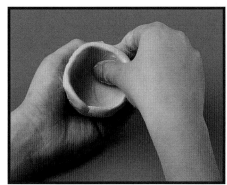

Rolling coils

You can use long clay sausages (coils) to build pots of any size and shape. The coils are made by rolling out the clay with your hands. For small pots, coils need to be about the thickness of your finger – make them a bit thicker for larger pots.

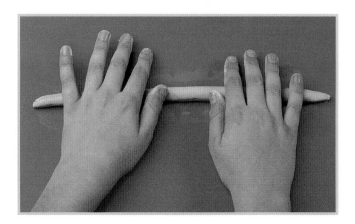

Making slabs

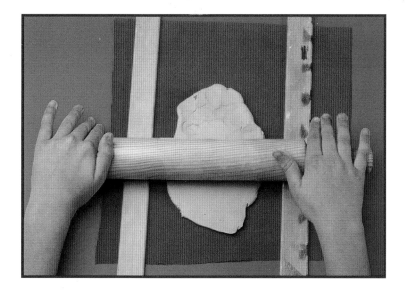

Flat slabs of clay can be used for tiles or for building boxes and containers. You will need a piece of cotton cloth (old cotton sheeting is ideal), a rolling pin and two lengths of wood. Place a ball of clay between the wooden lengths and flatten it with the rolling pin. The thickness of the wood controls the thickness of the slab.

Note It is much easier to roll out several small slabs than to try and roll out one huge one.

Cutting out shapes

Use a paper pattern and a knife to cut out your design. Leave the clay to harden slightly before moving it, otherwise you may distort the shape.

You can use pastry cutters to make fun shapes which you can stick on to your pots.

⚠ Knives are sharp. Ask an adult to help you cut out the shapes.

Creating patterns

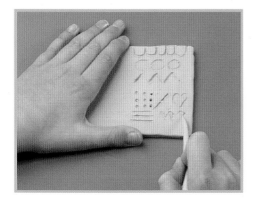

Wonderful patterns can be made in slabs of soft clay by rolling the clay over textured cloth or leaves, for example. Designs can be scratched into the surface with a modelling tool, the end of a pencil or even a stick. You can also impress objects into the clay to make patterns.

Joining and attaching

When joining coils or attaching small pieces of clay to larger pieces, the clay surfaces should be scored then moistened with water before being pressed and smoothed together. Allow all slab pieces to harden slightly first, so that they can be handled without losing their shape.

Note Pieces of air drying clay can be glued together with strong adhesive if you decide you want to add something to your model or pot after it is dry.

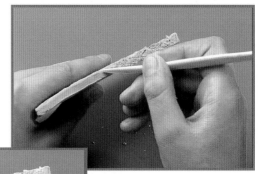

1 Use a modelling tool to score (roughen) all the edges to be joined.

2 Moisten the scored edges with a damp sponge.

3 Press the two edges together firmly, then use your fingers or a modelling tool to smooth the joins.

4 Finally, use a damp sponge on large pieces to create a really smooth finish.

Drying and painting

Before you paint your model, allow it to dry completely. The manufacturer's instructions will tell you how long you should wait, although it does depend on how warm your working environment is. If it is cold or damp, the drying time will be longer. Some instructions may tell you that you can speed up the process by drying the clay in the oven. This will harden the clay completely and make it more durable, but only do this if the instructions say so, and always get an adult to use the oven for you.

Acrylic paints are used for all the projects in this book. Poster paints can also be used, but you will need to seal them with acrylic varnish. The colours can be sponged on or you can use a brush to paint patterns and add fine details. An old toothbrush is ideal for spattering paint over surfaces. This creates lots of interesting effects, especially if you use several different colours.

Note Acrylic paints dry very quickly and paintbrushes and sponges must be cleaned immediately after use or they will be ruined.

Wobbly Pot

The pinching technique can be used to make a simple pinch pot like the one featured in this project. Throughout time, and in many different cultures, this style of pot has been used for various purposes. A good example is the diva pot used to hold small lights during the Hindu festival of Diwali.

YOU WILL NEED
Air-drying clay
Sponge
Modelling tool
Acrylic paints
Paintbrushes

Use the pinching technique (see page 8) to create a simple pot shape.

Squeeze the top of the pot to create a wavy edge. Leave it for half an hour to dry slightly.

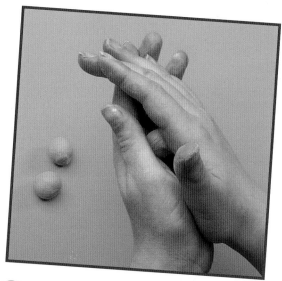

Roll three small balls of clay.

Score and moisten the surfaces to be joined (see page 10), then gently press each ball on to the base of the pot to form 'feet'. Smooth around the joins with a modelling tool. Leave to dry (see page 11).

5

Use a sponge to add large wavy stripes of paint around the pot.

6

Dip a stiff paintbrush or old toothbrush into acrylic paint, then hold it over the pot and rim and pull back the bristles with your finger. This will create a spattered paint effect. Wash your hands immediately afterwards.

FURTHER IDEAS

You can make wide and narrow pots – egg cups too. Decorate them with spots, stars or diamonds.

Fat Cat

In this project, coils of clay are used to make the collar, flower and tail for the cat. The eyes and ears are pinched out of small amounts of clay. Animal sculptures by the artist Picasso could be used as inspiration. You can model lots of animals by just squeezing and stretching the basic pinch pot. The cat can be changed into a penguin or a mouse in an instant!

YOU WILL NEED
Air-drying clay
Sponge
Modelling tool
Acrylic paints
Paintbrushes

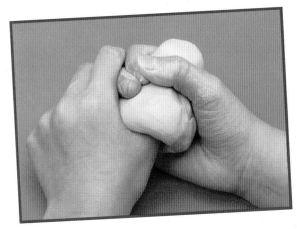

1 Make a basic pinch pot (see page 12). Turn it upside down and gently shape the head with your thumb.

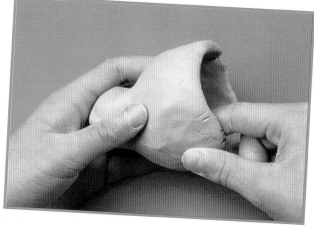

2 Squeeze the sides of the body, making it fatter than the head. Shape a nose and cheeks, then press in two eye sockets.

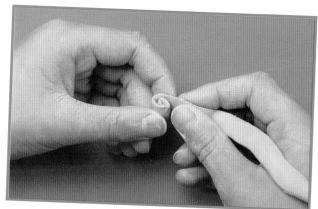

3 Roll out a coil of clay (see page 8) then flatten one end. Loosely spiral the flattened clay then pinch one end to form a flower head. Break off the flower then neaten the edge. Use the rest of the clay to make a collar and tail from coils, then two eyes and ears.

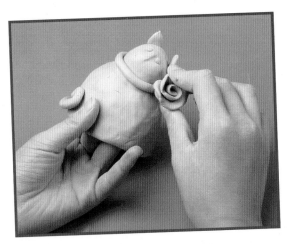

4 Attach the eyes, ears, tail and collar to the cat then add the flower to the collar (see page 10).

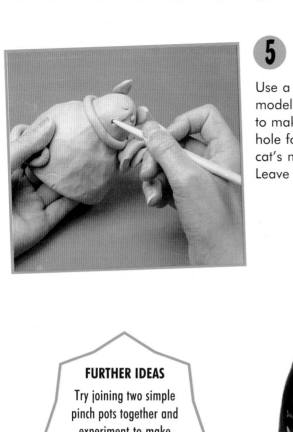

5

Use a pointed modelling tool to make a neat hole for the cat's mouth. Leave to dry.

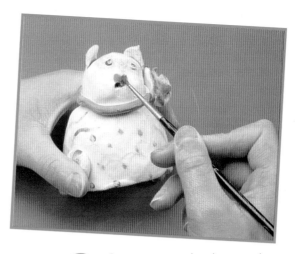

6

Sponge on a background colour and then use a paintbrush to add patterns to the body, the collar and the facial features.

FURTHER IDEAS

Try joining two simple pinch pots together and experiment to make other interesting animal models.

Swinging Tiger

Fun models like this tiger can be made from a solid lump of clay. Instead of pinching the clay into a pot shape, you simply roll it out and then pull out the arms and legs. Remember that the more clay you use, the longer it will take to dry. The smooth, pinched shapes of these models resemble the shapes of some African and Mexican sculpted creatures.

YOU WILL NEED
Air-drying clay
Modelling tool
Sponge • Acrylic paints
Paintbrushes
String or garden wire

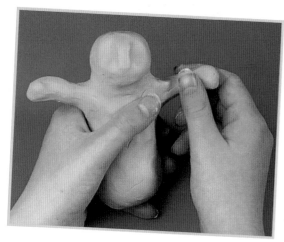

1 Roll out a fat clay sausage, shape a head and nose, then carefully pull two arms out from the sides of the body.

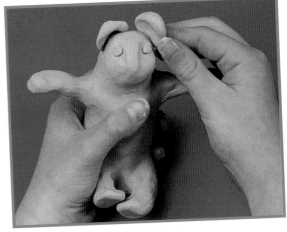

2 Model the bottom of the body and pull the legs out towards you. Add the eyes and ears.

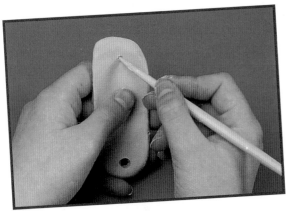

3 Model the swing seat from a slab of clay. Use the point of the modelling tool to make two small holes for the string or garden wire.

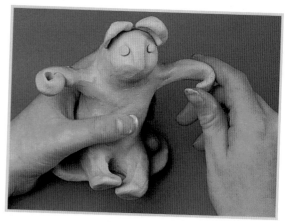

4 Attach the tiger to the seat. Bend the ends of its arms to form hands, leaving a hole in the middle of each for the string or garden wire to be pulled through. Leave to dry.

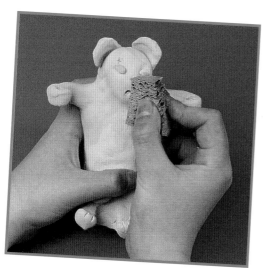

6

Thread the string or garden wire through the hands and seat, then knot the ends.

5 Sponge paint all over the model, then add stripes and facial features using a paintbrush.

FURTHER IDEAS

Try making your pet or even your best friend using this technique. You can add hair and facial features for people, then paint on colourful clothes.

Flower Pot

The technique of coiling is ideal for building up round symmetrical shapes like these flower pots. If you want your pot to be perfectly even, it is important to keep the coils the same thickness, and to continually turn the pot as you join and smooth the coils together. Look to artists and sculptors for ideas about what to paint on to or mould into the clay to decorate the flower pot. Inspiration for the flowers could be taken from famous paintings such as Van Gogh's 'Sunflowers'.

YOU WILL NEED

Air-drying clay
Modelling tool • Pastry cutter
Garden or florist's wire
Pebbles • Moss
Acrylic paints
Paintbrushes

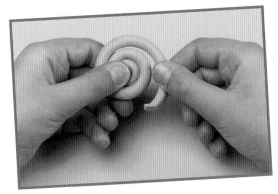

1 Roll out a coil of clay and use it to make a base. Smooth the coil flat.

2 Start to build up the walls of the pot using long, thin coils. Smooth the inside and outside surfaces with a modelling tool as you work upwards.

3 When the pot is tall enough, smooth the top of the rim, then use part of a pastry cutter to create a fancy edge.

4 Roll out a piece of clay and use the technique shown on page 14 to make small flower heads. Squeeze pieces of clay between your fingers and model them to form longer flower heads.

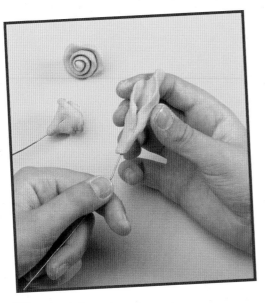

6 Paint the flowers, stems and pot then leave to dry. Arrange the flowers in the pot and use small pebbles to hold the wire stems in position. Finally, cover the top of the pebbles with some moss.

5 Push lengths of garden or florist's wire into each flower head then leave to dry.

FURTHER IDEAS
Air-drying clay is not waterproof, but you could build up the coils around a small glass jar, so you can then fill it with water and real flowers.

Squiggly Bowl

Coil pots used to be made by ancient cultures such as Native Americans. The coils provide an instant decoration which can then be painted in vivid colours. By using different thicknesses of coil and varying the shape of the coil you can experiment to produce different patterns and textures. In this project, a bowl lined with clingfilm acts as a mould, and coils are built up on the inside of the bowl. You can use any shape as a mould, provided that the top is wider than its base so that it is easy to remove the finished piece.

1 Line the inside of the mould with clingfilm, then lay squiggles and coils of clay inside the bowl.

2 Join all the coils together by gently smoothing the inside surface with your fingers. Do not press too hard, as you want the coil pattern to remain on the outside.

3 Lay two long coils of clay around the top of the bowl to form a rim. Allow the pot to harden slightly before removing it from the mould.

4 Make a base from long coils of clay. Smooth the inside of the coils together to make it stronger.

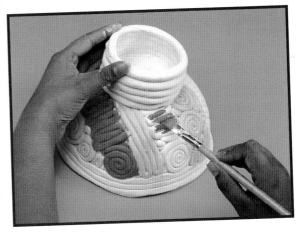

5 Turn the pot upside down and carefully attach the base (see page 10). Gently smooth the join with a modelling tool or your finger.

6 Allow the pot to dry completely, then paint the coils.

(see page 10)

FURTHER IDEAS

Make two bowls then place one on top of the other to make a person's head like the one shown here. You could also make a model of the Earth using this technique.

Fish Tile

The simple tile in this project is created by rolling the clay into a slab and then decorating it with cut-out shapes and paint. Look for different examples of tiles for inspiration. You may find them in your own home, or in most religious buildings. You can also look at the work of the Spanish artist, Gaudi, to see all the amazing things that can be done with tiles.

YOU WILL NEED
Air-drying clay
Knife • Rolling pin
Two lengths of wood • Sponge
Modelling tool • Acrylic paints
Paintbrushes • Scissors
Piece of wood

1

Photocopy the square, border, fish and wave patterns on page 31. Cut them out and then place them on a slab of clay. Use a knife to cut around the shapes then set them aside and allow to harden slightly. Roll a few tiny balls of clay to form bubbles.

Knives are sharp. Ask an adult to help you cut out the shapes.

2 Attach the border to the square base (see page 10). Smooth the edges of the joins with a modelling tool.

3 Use a sponge to smooth over the edges further, and to smooth over the front of the border.

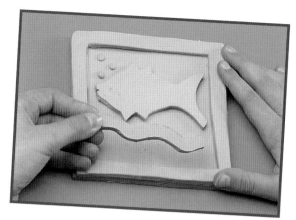

4 Attach all the pieces to the tile. Leave to harden slightly, then place a piece of wood on top to keep everything flat. Leave to dry thoroughly.

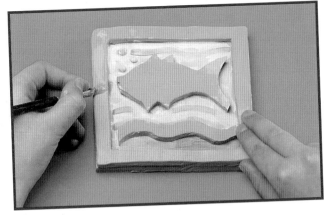

5 Paint the sea first, then apply a base colour to the fish, the wave and the border.

FURTHER IDEAS

You can use this technique to make a clock like the one shown here. Buy the clock mechanism first so that you know how big to make the hole in the clock face.

6 Use a paintbrush and different colours of paint to add details. Spatter on some speckles of paint with a stiff paintbrush or an old toothbrush.

Treasure Box

YOU WILL NEED

Air-drying clay
Knife • Rolling pin
Two lengths of wood
Modelling tool • Sponge
Acrylic paints
Paintbrushes

The decorations for this box are attached by scoring and moistening the two pieces of clay then joining them together. You could also explore other methods of decoration such as carving in shapes using modelling tools.

Photocopy the square patterns for the Treasure Box on page 31, then cut them out from slabs of clay. Allow the slabs to harden slightly then use a modelling tool to score the surfaces that will be joined.

(!)

Knives are sharp. Ask an adult to help you cut out the shapes.

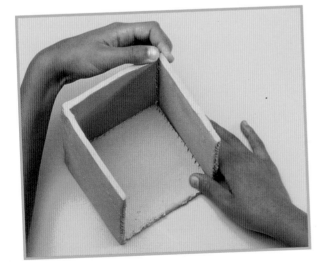

 Moisten the edges with a sponge then assemble the box as shown, with the scored edges touching one another. Leave off one side for the moment. Pinch and squash the clay pieces together then smooth over the outer joins.

3 Roll out long thin coils, then press and smooth these over the inside joins to strengthen them. Attach the remaining side then carefully strengthen that with a coil.

4 Join the two lid slabs together, then attach a long coil of clay around the outer edge. Smooth over the join. Turn the lid over.

5 Model a small animal (see pages 14–15) and attach it to the top of the lid with a thin coil. Smooth over the join.

6 Decorate the sides with coiled shapes, smoothing over the joins with a modelling tool. Let the box dry before painting it.

FURTHER IDEAS

You can convert this treasure box into a money box by cutting a slot in the lid before the clay dries.

Pencil Holder

Clay is an important material in the production of practical items, as well as being useful for producing decorative ornaments. The techniques used in this project are the same as those for the Treasure Box on pages 24–25, but the joins are strengthened on the outside rather than the inside.

YOU WILL NEED
Air-drying clay
Knife • Rolling pin
Two lengths of wood
Modelling tool
Pastry cutters • Sponge
Acrylic paints
Paintbrushes

1 Photocopy the patterns on page 30, then cut them out from slabs of clay. Allow the slabs to harden slightly, then assemble the triangle and three rectangles to form the basic pot shape.

! Knives are sharp. Ask an adult to help you cut out the shapes.

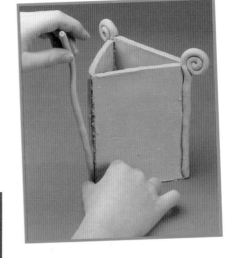

2 Roll out three long coils of clay, then smooth them on to the outside edges to strengthen the holder.

3 Decorate one side of the pencil holder using thin coils of clay to create windows, roof tiles, a door and even a milk bottle on the doorstep.

4 Use a coil and small pieces of clay to add a sunflower on one of the other sides. Use a pointed modelling tool to add veins to the leaves and seeds to the flower head.

5 Use pastry cutters to cut out a moon and stars to decorate the third side.

6 Attach the car to the pot to complete the scene. Leave to dry, then paint the pot with bright colours.

FURTHER IDEAS

Make your own house, or create a whole village! Alternatively, make a big pot and use it to hold cooking utensils.

Lion Dish

Your imagination can really run wild with this dish. I show you how to make a lion, but all kinds of shapes can be produced to make a variety of fantastic creatures. Use a mixture of decorative techniques to finish it off, including moulding, attaching clay shapes or creating patterns using clay tools.

YOU WILL NEED
Air-drying clay
Rolling pin • Two lengths of wood
Mould (dish) • Clingfilm
Sponge • Modelling tool
Garlic press or sieve
Acrylic paints
Paintbrushes

1 Cover the mould with clingfilm. Roll out the clay, then lay it over the mould. Gently ease the clay down using a sponge.

2 Trim off excess clay with a modelling tool. Allow the clay dish to harden slightly, then remove it from the mould.

3 Model a head and tail then attach them to the rim of the dish. Shape two ears and attach them to the head. Smooth over the joins with your fingers.

4 Squeeze a ball of clay through a garlic press or sieve to create the lion's mane and tail.

5 Use a modelling tool to transfer the squeezed clay on to the end of the lion's tail and around his head. Press the strands down well. Model and attach four feet, then then leave the dish to dry.

6 Sponge paint all over the dish. Use a paintbrush to add decoration and to colour in any areas that are hard to reach with a sponge.

FURTHER IDEAS
Use jelly moulds to create interesting shapes!
Look at animal books for interesting colours and patterns.

Patterns

The patterns on these two pages are the size that I used them for the projects, but you can make them larger or smaller on a photocopier if you wish. Once you have photocopied the patterns, you can cut them out and then place them over your clay and cut around the outline with a knife.

Get an adult to help you photocopy the patterns.

You will also need an adult to help you cut out the clay shapes.

Patterns for the Pencil Holder featured on pages 26–27. You will need three rectangular slabs of clay, one triangular slab and one car shape.

Patterns for the Fish Tile featured on pages 22–23. You will need two large square slabs of clay. Use one whole square for the background of the tile. Make the border from the other by cutting out the small square. Cut the fish and wave shapes from the remaining clay.

Patterns for the Treasure Box featured on pages 24–25. You will need five large square slabs for the actual box, and one large and one small square slab for the lid.

Index